Christmas Means Jesus

MAIN IDEA:
Jesus was a special baby.

SHARING FAITH WITH YOUR CHILD
During Advent we take the time to prepare for the coming Savior. Preparing for the arrival of children takes many forms. I hope you remember your time of waiting and preparing for the arrival of your child. Now you have the opportunity to share a time of waiting with your child. While it may seem all the world is awaiting Santa Claus and gifts, you have the opportunity to engage in activities to draw your child to see Christ in Christmas.

Place this Bible Story card in your Bible to mark Luke 1:31. Open the Bible with your child. Point to the verse as you read the words. Encourage your child to say the words with you. Read the Bible story printed on this card. If you have child-friendly Nativity figures, use them to retell the story with your child's help. **Say:** "Mary will have baby Jesus. I have a baby, too. My baby is you!" Enjoy hugs together.

Pray: Thank you, God, for baby Jesus. Thank you, God, for (your child's name).

First Sunday of December

Good News From the Angel

"Mary," called the angel. "Mary, you will have a baby."

"A baby?" asked Mary.

"Yes, Mary, you will have a baby boy. You will name him Jesus."

Mary said, "My baby will be named Jesus!"

Christmas Means Jesus

MAIN IDEA:
Jesus was a special baby.

SHARING FAITH WITH YOUR CHILD
Families often gather during holidays. It may be difficult for family members to understand a toddler who may be reserved or even cranky around extended family. Ease your child into family gatherings. Share photographs of family you will be visiting with, use their names frequently, and add their names to your prayer time with your toddler. During visits, plan to give family members relaxed time to enjoy the marvelous child you are rearing.

Place this Bible Story card in your Bible to mark Luke 1:31. Open the Bible with your child. Point to the verse as you read the words. Share the Bible story.

Say: "Mary took a trip to visit Elizabeth. Families take trips to visit each other." Use a familiar song melody and your own words to sing about any visits you will be part of during this holiday season.

Pray: Thank you, God, for all loving grownups.

Second Sunday of December

Mary Visits Aunt Elizabeth

Aunt Elizabeth hugged Mary. "Mary, you are going to have a baby!"

"Yes," said Mary. "My baby will be named Jesus."

Mary and Elizabeth felt happy.

Mary said, "God cares for me, and I am very glad!"

Christmas Means Jesus

MAIN IDEA:
Jesus was a special baby.

SHARING FAITH WITH YOUR CHILD
Toddlers are often fascinated by babies. They are aware of not *being* babies as well. You can use this self-awareness in creating important play together. Use a stuffed animal or doll to play "care for baby" together. Take turns rocking and holding the doll. If you have cold weather in your area, use a blanket or dinner napkin to wrap the doll to keep it warm. Give your toddler praise for each caring gesture he or she makes during the game.

Place the Bible Story card in your Bible to mark Luke 1:31. With your child, open the Bible to the Picture Card. Read the Bible verse and share the story on the back of the card together. Use child-friendly Nativity figures to retell the story with your toddler's help. Show your child one of his or her baby pictures. Tell your child you are happy to care for him or her, just as Mary and Joseph were happy to care for baby Jesus.

Pray: Thank you, God, for baby Jesus. Amen.

Third Sunday of December

Jesus Is Born

Mary held her new baby. "See, Joseph? Here is baby Jesus."

Joseph smiled at Mary. Joseph held baby Jesus' hands. Mary and Joseph were happy to care for the new baby.

Mary dressed baby Jesus. Joseph said, "Here is a dry, warm bed for baby Jesus. We will stay the night."

Mary and Joseph were glad to be warm and safe. Mary and Joseph were glad to care for Jesus.

Christmas Means Jesus

MAIN IDEA:
Jesus was a special baby.

SHARING FAITH WITH YOUR CHILD
Excitement! The air itself seems charged with excitement during the Advent/Christmas season. As caregivers of young children, parents quickly become aware of the season's effect on their children. Plan ahead to do all you are able to keep to the routines important in the life of all toddlers. Be intentional with rest and active times, meals, and lap time. Remember to take care of your child by seeing to your own needs as well.

Place the Bible Story card in your Bible to mark Luke 1:31. With your child, open the Bible to the Picture Card. Point to the Bible verse on the card as you read it to your child. Share the story on the back of the card together. Provide child-friendly Nativity figures to retell the story.

Pray: Thank you, God, for baby Jesus.

Fourth Sunday of December

Welcome, Jesus!

Welcome, Baby Jesus!

See the star?

Welcome, Baby Jesus!

Hear the angels?

Welcome, Baby Jesus!

Tell the shepherds?

Welcome, Baby Jesus!

Here is the manger!

Welcome, Baby Jesus!

Jesus Grew and I Grow

MAIN IDEA:
God plans for us to grow.

SHARING FAITH WITH YOUR CHILD
If your child was baptized as an infant, your congregation took a vow to help him or her grow as a Christian. It is likely that the child will not remember the event, but you can help by showing your child pictures of the baptism and telling stories about that important day—who was there, what you wore, who baptized him or her.

As parents, we offer love and care, and we do so without price. We take part in God's nature as we care for our children. And as we do, we sow the seeds of understanding of how great God's love for us is.

Place the Bible Story card in your Bible to mark Luke 2:52. Look at baby photos of your child together. Ask your toddler to name the baby. **Say:** "Yes, this is baby____! This baby is you! You are growing so much." With your child, open the Bible to the Picture Card. Point to the Bible verse on the card as you read it to your child. Share the story on the back of the card together.

Pray: Thank you, God, for growing bigger.

First Sunday of January

Simeon Sees Jesus

Mary wraps baby Jesus carefully. Today is a special day! Today Mary and Joseph take Jesus to the Temple.

"Peace to you, Mary and Joseph," calls old Simeon.

"God's peace to you, Simeon," calls Joseph.

Simeon takes little Jesus in his arms.

"Bless you, little Jesus!" says Simeon. "When I see you, I know God keeps promises! I am happy that God keeps promises!"

Jesus Grew and I Grow

MAIN IDEA:
God plans for us to grow.

SHARING FAITH WITH YOUR CHILD
Toddlers learn a great deal by imitating the adults in their lives. They depend on our signs and words of approval. Use your praise generously. Being appreciated and celebrating accomplishments provides a sense of well-being for your child. Give your toddler more and more household tasks to do. And always remember to express your approval for a job well done. After all, your child is growing in mind, body, and spirit. Your confidence in your child's growing abilities builds his or her self-confidence.

Place the Bible Story card in your Bible to mark Luke 2:52. Ask your child to help you get ready to share Bible Story Time together. (Bring the Bible to a favorite chair, turn on a light, or do any other task to prepare.) With your child, open the Bible and read the verse. Share the story on the back of the card together.

Pray: Thank you, God, for all the things I can do.

Second Sunday of January

Jesus Helps

Jesus puts a heavy piece of wood in its place. "Jesus, you use your strong arms to help. Thank you," says Mary. "Joseph, see how strong Jesus is. He carries all the wood!"

Joseph looks at all the wood Jesus piled together. "You are growing stronger every day!" said Joseph.

Jesus Grew and I Grow

MAIN IDEA:
God plans for us to grow.

SHARING FAITH WITH YOUR CHILD
Young children appreciate routine. Knowing what happens next contributes to their sense of security and confidence. Make preparing for going to church together part of your family's routine. Choose tasks your toddler can do to help. For example, you may ask your child to put his or her shoes in a special place before bedtime, or to put a toy or healthful snack in the bag you take to church. For children who have difficulty parting from time to time, focus on how the child is helping and then celebrate that work.

Place the Bible Story card in your Bible to mark Luke 2:52. With your child, open the Bible to the Picture Card. Point to the Bible verse on the card as you read it to your child. Share the story on the back of the card together. Play an "I Can Do" game together. **Say:** "I can clap (*clap hands 2 times*); so can you! I can stretch (*reach up high*); so can you! I can turn (*turn around*); so can you!"

Pray: Thank you, God, for all the things I can do. Thank you, God, for Sunday school.

Third Sunday of January

Going on a Trip

"What are you doing, Mother?" asked Jesus.

"I am preparing food for our journey, Jesus," said Mary.

"Where are we going?" asked Jesus.

"Tomorrow we will go to Jerusalem," said Joseph. "We will go to the House of the Lord, Jesus."

Jesus clapped his hands for joy. "Yes! I will go to the House of the Lord!"

Jesus Grew and I Grow

MAIN IDEA:
God plans for us to grow.

SHARING FAITH WITH YOUR CHILD
Parents of toddlers and twos have a daunting task: allowing the child to explore and learn while keeping the world pleasant and safe. Speed, curiosity, and the desire to imitate may lead a young child to explore medicine, knives, or other not-safe-for-twos objects. Use words to show danger. Try the phrase "not for you" instead of "no." Call things that are off-limits "Mommy's" or "Daddy's." ("Not for you. Mommy's knife.") Rely on words rather than on strong emotion to convey your message; it will maintain a sense of order and well-being for you and your child.

Place the Bible Story card in your Bible to mark Luke 2:52. Bring a shoe or bootie your child wore as an infant. Show it to your child. **Say:** "Oh, look how small your foot was when you were a baby." If your child is interested, try the shoe on your child and admire how much he or she has grown. With your child, open the Bible to the Picture Card. Read the verse and share the story together.

Pray: Thank you, God, for how we grow.

Fourth Sunday of January

New Sandals

"Too small," says Jesus.

"Your sandals are too small, Jesus." Joseph looks at Jesus' foot. "You are growing!"

"Yes, I am growing," said Jesus. "But my sandals are not growing."

"We will get bigger sandals for a growing boy's feet," said Joseph.

Jesus Grew

MAIN IDEA:
Jesus grew just as I grow.

SHARING FAITH WITH YOUR CHILD
The first step in faith growth for toddlers and twos is when adults, particularly parents, pay attention to the child's needs. All good parents seek to respond in good time to the needs of toddlers to be changed, to be fed, to be rocked, to be talked to, and to be played with.

Such actions say to the child, "This person cares for me." The actions build the foundation for the child to be able to say, "I know what it is like for God to care for me, because I have experienced care from adults who care for me."

During these first few years of your child's life, his or her brains are learning to trust. If the child is not exposed to loving care during the first few years of life, chances are he or she will never learn to trust in God, in Jesus, or in any other person or system. Teach your child that he or she is first and foremost a beloved child of God.

Pray: Thank you, God, for loving me.

Winter Fifth Sunday

Jesus Grows

"Waah, waah," cried baby Jesus. Mary rocked him quietly back to sleep.

"I like the stars," said the little boy Jesus to his father, Joseph.

"I can help sweep for you," said the big boy Jesus in his father's carpenter shop.

"Love one another," said the grown-up Jesus to his friends.

Jesus Loves the Children

MAIN IDEA:
Jesus loves little children.

SHARING FAITH WITH YOUR CHILD
Coming–going, up–down, here–there, front–back. At age two, your child has acquired many language skills. Opposites may seem magnetic to your child. Light switches for on and off, hands that open and shut, and toys that stop and go all explain how these pairs of words operate in our language. In your prayer time, reflect with thanksgiving and awe on the amazing growth you witness in your child.

Place the Bible Story card in your Bible at Mark 10:14. Bring toy people and a box with a removable lid to your Bible story place. Open the box lid. **Say:** "People in the box." Place the toy people in the box with your child's help. Close the box. **Ask:** "Where are the people?" Open the box and remove the people, saying, "People out of the box." Open the Bible to the Picture Card. Point to the Bible verse on the card as you read it to your child. Share the story on the back of the card together.

Pray: Thank you, God, for coming and going.

Second Sunday of February

Jesus Loves Me

Coming–going, coming–going.

People hurry to see Jesus.

Coming–going, coming–going.

Is there room for one more friend?

Coming–going, coming–going.

Is there room for one small friend?

Coming–going, coming–going.

Jesus welcomes little me!

Jesus Loves the Children

MAIN IDEA:
Jesus loves little children.

SHARING FAITH WITH YOUR CHILD
Repetition is an important anchor for our young children. Building upon familiar activities and songs allows the toddler to move beyond what is familiar without losing his or her sense of security. During the routines of dressing, household tasks, mealtimes, and play times, build on the routine and the expected by adding new tasks or activities.

Young children thrive on repetition. How many times does your child ask for a particular favorite book? One of the first words toddlers learn to use is "Again!"

Place the Bible Story card in your Bible at Mark 10:14. With your child, open the Bible to the Picture Card. Point to the Bible verse on the card as you read it to your child. Share the story on the back of the card together.

Pray: Thank you, God, for loving me.

Third Sunday of February

Jesus Loves Micah

"Micah, Micah," Leah calls to her friend.

"Here I am, Leah," says Micah.

"Micah, Jesus is calling for little children. Come with me to Jesus!"

Micah smiles. "Yes! I will come. Jesus loves me!"

CHILD INFORMATION SHEET

Today's date: _____

Full name of child: _____

Name child is called: _____

Date of birth: _____

Is child baptized? _____ Yes _____ No

Address: _____

Home phone: _____

Mother's name: _____

Address: _____

Home phone: _____

Work phone: _____

Cell phone: _____

E-mail: _____

Father's name: _____

Address: _____

Home phone: _____

Work phone: _____

Cell phone: _____

E-mail: _____

Who lives in the home with the child?
    (Name, relationship to child, age)

_____

_____

_____

Has the child been in group care before?

_____ Yes _____ No

If yes, where? _____

Was this group care a positive experience?

_____ Yes _____ No

Explain: _____

_____

_____

Does the child take regular naps?
If yes, what are his or her regular nap times?

_____

Does the child have allergies?

_____

_____

Is the child on any kind of regular medication?

_____ Yes _____ No   If yes, describe:

_____

Is your child toilet trained? _____ Yes _____ No

What are the words your child uses for toileting?

_____

Describe some of the activities your child enjoys:

_____

_____

_____

What words would you use to describe your child?

_____

_____

Is there anything else your child's teachers need to know to best meet the needs of your child?

_____

_____

_____

_____

From *The First Three Years: A Guide for Ministry With Infants, Toddlers, and Two-Year-Olds.*
Copyright © 1995, 2001 Discipleship Resources.